Manitoba

Manitoba

Sarah Yates

Lerner Publications Company

LIBRARY OF CONGRESS
CATALOGING-IN-PUBLICATION DATA

Yates, Sarah.
  Manitoba / by Sarah Yates.
    p. cm.—(Hello Canada)
  Includes index.
  ISBN 0-8225-2756-1 (lib. bdg.)
  1. Manitoba—Juvenile literature. [1. Manitoba.] I. Title. II. Series.
F1062.4.Y38 1996   95-4223
971.27—dc20   CIP
                                       AC

Manufactured in the United States of America
1 2 3 4 5 6 – JR – 01 00 99 98 97 96

Cover photograph by Brian Sytnyk/Vis-U-Tel Photography. Background photo by R. Chen/Super Stock.

The glossary that begins on page 72 gives definitions of words shown in **bold type** in the text.

Senior Editor
Gretchen Bratvold
Editor
Lori Coleman
Photo Researcher
Cindy Hartmon Nelson
Series Designer
Steve Foley

Our thanks to the following people for their help in preparing this book: Dr. E. Leigh Syms, Curator of Archaeology, Manitoba Museum of Man and Nature, and Donna Stewart, Native Affairs Secretariat, Government of Manitoba.

 This book is printed on acid-free, recyclable paper.

Contents

Fun Facts

🍁 If you've ever wondered how the famous bear Winnie-the-Pooh got his funny name, ask a Winnipegger. The storybook character was named after a live bear who once lived in a zoo in England. The real bear's owner, who missed his hometown of Winnipeg, Manitoba, called the animal Winnie.

🍁 When the Winnipeg Blue Bombers won the Grey Cup in 1935, they became the first football club west of the Ontario border to take the national championship.

🍁 Manitoba records Canada's greatest temperature difference between winter and summer. With temperatures as low as −40° F (−40° C) in winter and as high as 104° F (40° C) some summers, Manitobans may see the temperature swing 144° F (80° C) in one year!

Hi! My name is Barkley. As you read *Manitoba*, I will be helping you make sense of some of the maps and charts that appear in the book.

In 1870 Manitoba was so small it was called the Postage Stamp Province. The boundaries were extended in 1881, in 1884, and in 1912—the year that Manitoba's present borders were set.

The Royal Canadian Mint in Winnipeg, the capital of Manitoba, makes all of Canada's coins.

Every spring at the Narcisse Snake Dens in Narcisse, Manitoba, you can watch thousands of garter snakes slither out of cracks in the rocks to mate.

The town of Churchill, Manitoba, is known as the Polar Bear Capital of the World. Here, along the shores of Hudson Bay, dozens of polar bears gather each fall to hunt seals.

Land of the Great Spirit

Manitoba takes its name from *manito waba,* an Aboriginal phrase meaning "place where the Great Spirit whispers." The whispering sound happens when waves hit the shore along an island in Lake Manitoba, a large body of water in the southern part of the province. The Native peoples said the Great Spirit Manito—who was present in the water, the land, and all things—made the sound. Through Manito, people felt a close connection to the natural world. Nowadays, many Manitobans share a similar respect for their homeland.

Waves (facing page) *lap against the rocky shoreline of Lake Manitoba. Bright red arctic bearberry* (above) *thrives in the cold climate of northern Manitoba.*

9

Located midway between the Pacific Ocean to the west and the Atlantic Ocean to the east, Manitoba is nicknamed the Keystone Province. In an arch, a keystone is the center piece of an arch that links the structure together and holds it up. Like a keystone, Manitoba connects eastern and western Canada. People from all over Canada meet for business in Winnipeg, Manitoba's capital.

In eastern Manitoba, evergreen forests mark the province's border with Ontario. In western Manitoba, rolling hills and **prairie,** or grasslands, cross into neighboring Saskatchewan. To the north are the Northwest Territories and

The city of Winnipeg is home to more than half of all Manitobans.

the icy coast of Hudson Bay. To the south lie the U.S. states of North Dakota and Minnesota. Manitoba is large enough to hold three states the size of Minnesota and is nearly one-third the size of the country of Mexico.

Manitoba is the farthest east of Canada's three Prairie Provinces, which include Saskatchewan and Alberta. Together, these three provinces form a vast expanse of dry grassland with few trees.

A buffalo and her calf munch prairie grass in Riding Mountain National Park in western Manitoba. Herds of buffalo once ran freely on the prairies, but nowadays much of the land is farmed.

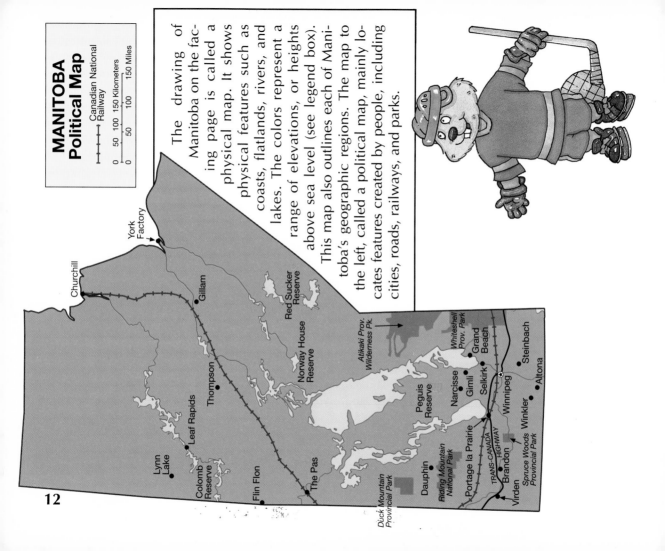

MANITOBA Political Map

Canadian National Railway

0 50 100 150 Kilometers
0   50   100   150 Miles

The drawing of Manitoba on the facing page is called a physical map. It shows physical features such as coasts, flatlands, rivers, and lakes. The colors represent a range of elevations, or heights above sea level (see legend box). This map also outlines each of Manitoba's geographic regions. The map to the left, called a political map, mainly locates features created by people, including cities, roads, railways, and parks.

York Factory

Churchill

Gillam

Red Sucker Reserve

Atikaki Prov. Wilderness Pk.

Whiteshell Prov. Park

Thompson

Leaf Rapids

Norway House Reserve

Grand Beach

Steinbach

Lynn Lake

Colomb Reserve

Flin Flon

The Pas

Peguis Reserve

Narcisse

Gimli

Selkirk

Winnipeg

Winkler

Altona

Dauphin

Riding Mountain National Park

Portage la Prairie

TRANS-CANADA HIGHWAY

Brandon

Virden

Spruce Woods Provincial Park

Duck Mountain Provincial Park

12

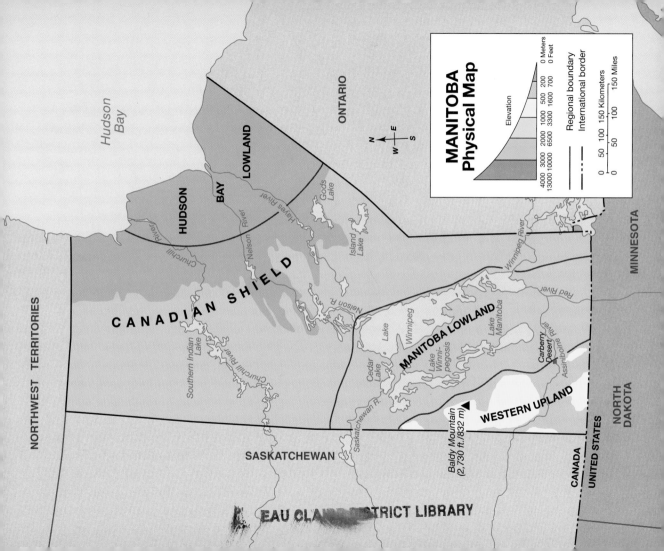

Hudson
Bay

ONTARIO

HUDSON BAY LOWLAND

HUDSON BAY

Haves River

Gods Lake

Churchill River

Nelson River

Island Lake

CANADIAN SHIELD

NORTHWEST TERRITORIES

Southern Indian Lake

Churchill River

Nelson R.

Saskatchewan R.

SASKATCHEWAN

Cedar Lake

Lake Winnipeg

Lake Winnipegosis

MANITOBA LOWLAND

Lake Manitoba

Winnipeg River

Red River

MINNESOTA

Carberry Desert

Assiniboine River

WESTERN UPLAND

Baldy Mountain
(2,730 ft./832 m)

NORTH DAKOTA

CANADA
UNITED STATES

MANITOBA Physical Map

Elevation

Meters	Feet
0	0
200	700
500	1600
1000	3300
2000	6500
3000	10000
4000	13000

Regional boundary
International border

0   50   100   150 Kilometers
0   50   100   150 Miles

N E S W

People say you can see forever on the prairies of southern Manitoba, where the sky stretches on and on and sunsets last for hours. At night, **northern lights** (aurora borealis) form yellow, green, and red bands that dance like a light show across Manitoba's great expanse of sky.

Thousands of years ago, during the **Ice Age,** Manitoba was covered by **glaciers,** or thick, slow-moving sheets of ice. The climate eventually warmed, melting the glaciers. This meltwater formed Lake Agassiz, which once sprawled across much of Manitoba. When this ancient lake slowly began to

One of Manitoba's many rivers rushes down a hillside, forming a glistening waterfall.

dry up, it left behind the province's three largest lakes—Winnipeg, Manitoba, and Winnipegosis. More than 100,000 smaller lakes in the province—including Cedar, Southern Indian, Island, and Gods—were also created by glaciers.

Manitoba is divided into four geographic regions. The Canadian Shield separates the Hudson Bay Lowland in the north from two other regions in the south—the Manitoba Lowland and the Western Upland.

Orr Lake is just one of thousands of small lakes in northern Manitoba. So many bodies of water dot the province that some have never even been named.

15

Running right through the middle of the province, the Canadian Shield covers three-fifths of Manitoba. This huge region also extends across much of Canada and contains some of the world's oldest rock. In Manitoba, the rock holds valuable minerals such as nickel, zinc, and gold.

Marshes, moss-covered rocks, and thick evergreen forests cover the Shield. The lonely birdcall of the loon haunts summer evenings on cool, clear lakes. The Shield is also home to moose, bears, and beavers. Communities in the region include Flin Flon, Lynn Lake, The Pas, and Thompson—Manitoba's third largest city.

Where the rugged Canadian Shield meets the Hudson Bay Lowland to the northeast, moose, wolves, and caribou roam through large evergreen forests.

A moose wanders through the woodlands of northern Manitoba.

Stunted evergreen trees struggle to grow in the northern tundra.

Closer to the bay, the forests give way to spongy wetlands, or **muskegs.** In warm weather, many parts of this land can't be crossed on foot without sinking into ankle-deep mush.

Beneath this spongy land is **permafrost,** a layer of ground that is frozen all year. The only plants that survive in the thin layer of soil that covers the permafrost are stunted trees with shallow roots and mosses and lichens—plants formed by algae and fungi. This frozen, almost treeless flatland is called **tundra**.

Along the shores of Hudson Bay, tides carry this salty sea as far as three miles (five kilometers) inland, during the months the water is not frozen. When the tide rolls back to sea, boats run aground with no water in sight. Thousands of beluga whales mate in Hudson Bay. Each October polar bears jump onto huge chunks of floating ice to hunt seals in the bay.

In spring, the ice in Hudson Bay breaks up into thousands of chunks (left), *some of which are stranded on shore* (above) *when the tide moves out to sea.*

The Assiniboine River winds through western Winnipeg before joining the Red River in the heart of the city.

Another lowland region—called the Manitoba Lowland—extends southwest from the Canadian Shield. Most of the Manitoba Lowland is flat or gently rolling forestland. More than half of all Manitobans live in this region, especially around the city of Winnipeg. Located at the forks of two major rivers—the Red and the Assiniboine—the capital is a hub of manufacturing, shipping, and government. The Manitoba Lowland is also home to the province's three largest lakes. Thousands of birds, including Canada geese, grebes, mallards, and piping plovers, nest near the shores.

West of Lakes Manitoba and Winnipegosis is a sharp rise in the landscape known as an **escarpment.** This rise marks the beginning of Manitoba's fourth region—the Western Upland. Beyond the escarpment, rolling prairies with rich soil contain some of Manitoba's best farmland.

19

An unusual part of the Upland is the Carberry Desert, with its cactuses and sand dunes. These hills of sand, silt, and gravel were left by a glacier thousands of years ago. Nearby is Brandon—the second largest city in the province. South of the city, steep oak-covered slopes and long narrow lakes attract large groups of pelicans.

The Assiniboine River flows east across the Western Upland and the Manitoba Lowland before joining the Red River in Winnipeg. Three major rivers—the Red, the Saskatchewan, and the Winnipeg—drain into Lake Winnipeg. The principal northern rivers are the Nelson, Churchill, and Hayes. All of Manitoba's rivers eventually empty into Hudson Bay.

Near the bay, the weather is chilly year-round. In Churchill, for example,

The Spirit Sands, a stretch of sand dunes in southern Manitoba, are also known as the Carberry Desert. Besides cactuses and hardy grasses and trees, desert-dwelling snakes and lizards thrive in the sands.

the average temperature in January is an icy −18° F (−28° C), and in July it only reaches 54° F (12° C). Temperatures are warmer and winters are shorter in the south. In Winnipeg, for example, the January average is −2° F (−19° C), and the July average is 68° F (20° C). Manitoba's typically bright, sunny skies occasionally give way to short, heavy showers. Average **precipitation** (rain and melted snow) is about 20 inches (51 centimeters) a year.

When it comes to climate, Manitoba is a land of amazing contrasts. Temperatures differ greatly between winter and summer and between north and south. But the changes in weather seem to fit a province whose landscape changes from an icy north shore, to a heartland of ancient rock, to miles of rolling prairie.

In some parts of Manitoba, winter temperatures may hang below freezing for more than six months a year.

21

First Nations and Fur Traders

The first people in what is now Manitoba were the Aboriginals, or North American Indians, who probably arrived from the southwest around 8500 B.C. These Native peoples, ancestors of Canada's First Nations groups, lived and traveled in family bands of 25 to 30 people. To survive they hunted huge woolly mammoths and giant bison (buffalo) and gathered a variety of plants.

Gradually, these large animals died out. Aboriginals then began tracking smaller buffalo, caribou, elk, and deer. These grazing herds moved with the seasons, and hunter families followed. Food was plentiful some years. Other years could be very hard. Floods, storms, and other natural events sometimes blocked the routes of the animal herds and kept them from crossing the paths of hunters.

A turtle design made with large stones lies near Betula Lake in Whiteshell Provincial Park. This form and other nearby fish and bird designs were created hundreds of years ago by Native peoples.

Digging into the Past

The forks of the Red and Assiniboine Rivers have been a popular meeting place for more than 6,000 years. People long ago traveled here by river every year to trade, hunt, and fish. They also feasted and celebrated among friends and relatives. Afterward, they left behind traces of their visit—ashes from campfires, bones from the food eaten, and small fragments of tools and jewelry. Each time the rivers flooded, a layer of sand, silt, or clay covered these pieces from the past, preserving them for the future.

Nowadays, as part of The Forks Public Archaeology Project, people from ages 8 to 90 work on their hands and knees alongside professional archaeologists. Together they dig up the past. Layers of ground each represent a "living floor." At this site, the layers include an ancient Native camp, forts, farms and towns.

The deepest layer is a 3,000-year-old Native campsite. To reach this level, workers use a backhoe to dig a deep pit. Then soil is removed with hand shovels and trowels. Using string, the ground is sectioned into squares. Everybody works a square. They use teaspoons, grapefruit knives, even dental picks to remove the soil around the artifacts.

Many of the objects uncovered give clues to ancient trade networks. Diggers have found tools made of stone from places as far away as western North Dakota, South Dakota, the western Great Lakes, and even Texas!

For ages, the rivers brought traders to the site, provided food, and eventually covered all trace of activity. Explains Sid Kroker, the archaeologist in charge, "Every time you dig, you raise more questions than you answer. It's like a jigsaw puzzle without a picture—without even the edges. A more complete picture is put together as you uncover more."

Aboriginal hunters used snowshoes to hunt buffalo and other game in winter.

Families traveled great distances on foot, carrying their possessions. Dogs pulled some goods on wooden frames called travois. By 1000 B.C., these early peoples were trading regularly with Aboriginal groups from other areas.

By A.D. 1200, the early Manitobans were exchanging furs, meat, and fish for corn, beans, sunflower seeds, and tobacco. Traders learned many new skills through their contact with other groups. For example, people in what is now Manitoba began to make pottery and to craft tools from obsidian, a black rock. They began growing corn and, eventually, riding horses to hunt buffalo. Later, trade with European newcomers changed Aboriginal lifeways forever.

When Europeans first arrived in Manitoba in the 1600s, there were four main groups of Aboriginals. Each group lived on a different type of land. In each region, the people had learned to adapt their ways to the climate, plants, and animals around them.

On the dry, grassy plains of the, southwest, the Nakota (or Assiniboine) and the Plains Cree depended on buffalo for almost everything. From buffalo skins these and other Plains Indians sewed clothing and tepees (cone-shaped dwellings). People carved tools and needles from buffalo bones. They dried buffalo manure to use as fuel for fires. And from buffalo flesh, Plains Indians made pemmican, a long-lasting mixture of dried meat, animal fat, and ground berries.

In the forests of southeastern and central Manitoba, people found a wide variety of plants and animals. The Woodland Cree and the Saulteaux constructed dome-shaped wigwams from saplings covered with tree bark, rush mats, and animal skins. They hunted moose, bears, and beavers. They also harvested wild rice and other plants.

To the north, where the forests thin out into tundra, groups such as the Swampy Cree and the Chipewyan (or Dene) made wigwams and caribou-skin tepees for shelter. These subarctic peoples hunted caribou, arctic fox, ducks, and geese and used plants for many things. For example, sphagnum moss from local muskegs was used for diapers and for wiping.

In the frozen land of the far north, life was harsh. Here the Inuit fished and hunted polar bears, seals, whales, and caribou, but starvation was a common threat. People carved blocks of ice to build winter homes. In summer they lived in caribou-skin tepees.

Europeans first reached these frozen parts of what is now Manitoba in 1612. Searching for a way to cross North America by water, the British

A Cree hunter and his family scan the Hudson Bay landscape. The Cree traded animal pelts for many European goods, including guns. With guns, Native peoples could hunt more ducks, geese, and fur-bearing animals than before.

explorer Sir Thomas Button sailed into Hudson Bay and spent a winter at the mouth of the Nelson River. Button didn't find a way to cross the continent by water, but he did claim the land he found for Great Britain.

In 1670 the British king Charles II gave this huge territory to the Hudson's Bay Company—a British fur trading operation. The land was called Rupert's Land after the king's cousin. It included all of what is now Manitoba.

The Hudson's Bay Company planned to trap beavers and other fur-bearing animals in Rupert's Land and sell the pelts in Europe to make shiny black top hats, which were very popular. In 1682 the company built York Factory—the first trading post in what is now Manitoba—on the southwestern shore of Hudson Bay. Gradually, the company built a string of forts and trading posts throughout Rupert's Land.

Meanwhile, French explorers also wanted to find a route across North America. They sent the La Vérendrye family to explore Rupert's Land. The La Vérendryes never reached the Pacific Ocean, but they built several trading posts and forts, including Fort Rouge at the forks of the Red and Assiniboine. French fur traders soon came from Montréal to the east.

Members of the La Vérendrye expedition stop to camp at Lake of the Woods, on the southeastern tip of what is now Manitoba, and plan the next leg of their journey.

Many of the French and the British traders married Cree women. These women taught their husbands how to speak Aboriginal languages and how to survive the harsh winters. In turn, the men taught their wives about the Christian religion. The children of these marriages—known as Métis—grew up with two cultures. Most Métis families were Christian but they also kept many Aboriginal beliefs. The Métis farmed and lived in European-style homes. Some went on buffalo hunts and lived in tepees part of the year.

For 200 years, the European traders depended on Aboriginal and Métis trappers, who brought furs to the trading posts. The Métis also supplied pemmican and buffalo meat to the Europeans, many of whom worked for the North West Company. Set up in Montréal in the 1770s, this fur-trading firm competed with the Hudson's Bay Company.

A fur trader makes his way through the cold to a fort on Hudson Bay. Many fur traders—both French and British—married Native women.

Lord Selkirk founded the Red River Colony—the first permanent settlement in what is now Manitoba.

The rivalry between the two companies increased in the early 1800s. The Hudson's Bay Company, along with Scottish nobleman Thomas Douglas, earl of Selkirk, planned to start a farming **colony,** or settlement, right in the heart of North West Company operations. In 1812 Lord Selkirk brought a group of farmers from Scotland and Ireland to what became the Red River Colony, which was based at the forks of the Red and Assiniboine Rivers.

The North West Company and the local Métis grew angry. The Red River Colony threatened the North West Company's control of food supplies and trade routes in the region. Violence broke out near the forks at a place called Seven Oaks in 1816. Led by Cuthbert Grant, the Métis killed several colonists.

The disagreements continued until 1821, when the North West Company merged with the Hudson's Bay Company. The bigger firm gained control of the Red River Colony and ran it as a trading post, with headquarters at Fort Garry on the forks.

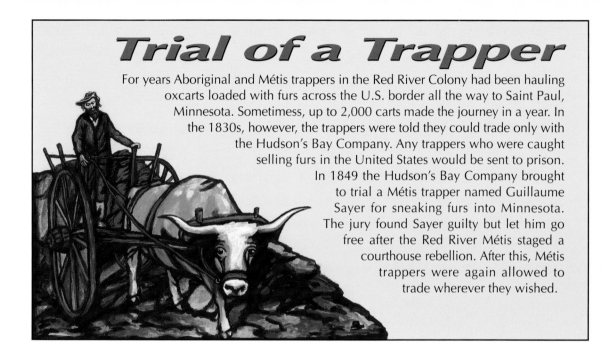

Trial of a Trapper

For years Aboriginal and Métis trappers in the Red River Colony had been hauling oxcarts loaded with furs across the U.S. border all the way to Saint Paul, Minnesota. Sometimess, up to 2,000 carts made the journey in a year. In the 1830s, however, the trappers were told they could trade only with the Hudson's Bay Company. Any trappers who were caught selling furs in the United States would be sent to prison. In 1849 the Hudson's Bay Company brought to trial a Métis trapper named Guillaume Sayer for sneaking furs into Minnesota. The jury found Sayer guilty but let him go free after the Red River Métis staged a courthouse rebellion. After this, Métis trappers were again allowed to trade wherever they wished.

Métis and colonists continued to live side by side at Red River. But life began to change in the mid-1800s. Top hats made from beaver pelts were no longer in fashion in Europe. As the fur trade slowed, the British owners of the Hudson's Bay Company gradually lost interest in Rupert's Land.

By the 1860s, the Red River Colony had more than 10,000 settlers, most of whom were Métis. As more and more newcomers came to farm, however, the Métis feared losing their land.

From Provincehood to the 21st Century

In 1867 the British North America Act created a new country called the Dominion of Canada, which included four provinces—Ontario, Québec, New Brunswick, and Nova Scotia. To increase the size of the Dominion, the new Canadian government bought Rupert's Land from Great Britain. Government officials wanted to measure and divide the new territory into lots on which settlers could build homes.

Canadian officials often treated the Métis unfairly.

Louis Riel worked hard to preserve French language and culture. He wanted to make sure the Métis had French schools, freedom of language and religion, and a voice in the Canadian government.

At Red River, the Métis worried that the government would move them off their land. In 1869 Métis leader Louis Riel organized a takeover of Fort Garry and set up a temporary government. He and other leaders wrote a list of Métis rights they wanted to protect. They sent the list to Ottawa, the Canadian capital.

After several months of bargaining with Riel, Canadian officials passed the Manitoba Act in 1870. Under the act, Manitoba became the fifth province of Canada. The ruling also granted most of the Métis' requests. In addition, the government upheld Métis land claims.

But Riel's joy over these gains was shortlived. Although he was twice elected to Manitoba's legislature, he was not allowed to serve. Riel fled to the United States to escape Canadian troops. Many of the settlers and soldiers sent to the new province were not friendly to the Métis. Little by little, they lost their land and other rights. More than two out of every three Métis in Manitoba eventually left, moving west and north.

First Nations people in the new province also saw drastic changes. Between 1871 and 1875, Manitoba claimed much of the land on which Aboriginals had traditionally hunted and lived. They were moved to settlements on parcels of land called **reserves.** Many reserves were too small for hunting, and the soil was often too poor to farm. Aboriginals were forced to depend on meager supplies from the government. The most fertile land in the province was now open to European **immigrants.**

In the 1870s, many farmers from neighboring Ontario moved to Manitoba. And a new group of immigrants—the Mennonites—arrived. They had left their farms on the prairies of Russia to find religious freedom. In Manitoba the Mennonites continued their

Canadian government officials and Native leaders met in 1871 at Lower Fort Garry to discuss a treaty. Through treaties, Aboriginals were forced to give away their homelands. In return, they got a very small yearly payment and were moved to reserves.

practice of planting shelterbelts—long rows of trees that kept the fertile soil from blowing away.

Icelanders also came to Manitoba in the 1870s. They set up a fishing and farming village on the shores of Lake Winnipeg. The newcomers named the village Gimli, which means "paradise" in the Icelandic language.

At the same time, farmers discovered new types of grain and better methods of grinding grain. Manitoba soon had extra wheat to sell outside the province, helping farmers make a profit. Still, farm life was not easy. Fierce winters, summer mosquitoes, and loneliness made the prairies a tough place to start a new life. At first, most new settlers built houses from blocks of sod—dirt and grass cut from the ground. Later, log, stone, and frame houses became common.

In 1885 immigrant workers completed a railroad across Canada. Many

A PIONEER DOCTOR

In 1881 David Ross purchased a sawmill in the small town of Whitemouth. He built a log cabin on the river and sent for his family to join him. He was proud to tell residents that his wife, a real doctor, would soon arrive.

Many of Dr. Charlotte Ross's patients were loggers with deep ax wounds. Sometimes she had to sew up a wound with an ordinary needle and thread. As news of her medicine spread, nearby Saulteaux Indians also came to her for healing.

As Whitemouth grew, Dr. Ross delivered many babies. She reached her patients by canoe, by oxcart, by horseback, or, in winter, by sleigh. After a baby was born, the doctor often stayed to scrub floors, do laundry, and cook enough food to last a few days. With eight children of her own, Charlotte Ross knew that families needed help with chores while mothers recovered from childbirth.

Members of an immigrant family stand outside their farm in southern Manitoba. Settlers came to the province from a wide range of places in the late 1800s and early 1900s.

of the laborers were Chinese, and some of them stayed in Manitoba. The new tracks made it easier and quicker for people to reach Manitoba. As more newcomers arrived, cities and towns sprang up along the railroad.

To attract still more immigrants, the Canadian government sent its minister of immigration—a Manitoban named Clifford Sifton—to Germany. There he advertised cheap farmland in the Canadian West. Thousands came, including Ukrainians and other eastern Europeans.

Many travelers passed through Winnipeg on their way west. Those who stayed turned Winnipeg into a modern trading center. Warehouses were built to store crops, and the city became a hub of trade in groceries. In 1887 merchants opened the Winnipeg Grain Exchange. Buyers and sellers met there to settle prices for grain and vegetable crops.

In 1906 workers completed a dam across the Winnipeg River. This wall made the water drop with great force, turning engines that generated electricity. Called **hydroelectric power,** this form of electricity was cheap because it required no fuel. Industries that needed a lot of electricity to run machinery were attracted to the area.

By 1913 Winnipeg was the third largest city in Canada. That year it peaked as a manufacturing, warehousing, and railroad center. Land prices boomed. A railway network spread in all directions from the city. Lumber and flour mills, meat-packing houses, coal yards, clothing factories, metal and machine shops all offered more jobs than people could fill.

Many Winnipeggers grew unhappy with low wages and long workdays. To protest against these conditions, nearly 30,000 city workers walked off the job during the Winnipeg General Strike. It began on May 15, 1919. For six weeks the city stood at a halt—streetcars, post offices, newspapers, and milk and bread deliveries all stopped. The city council hired the Royal Canadian Mounted Police to keep order. When the strike finally ended, little changed and workers were still angry.

Hard times continued in the 1930s, when a lack of rain dried up southern Manitoba's farmland and wind blew the dusty topsoil away. Crops failed. Farms and other businesses went bankrupt. All across Canada, people lost their jobs and homes during this period, known as the Great Depression.

Northern Manitoba was not hit as hard during the depression. Métis and

Angry citizens topple a streetcar during the Winnipeg General Strike.

Native workers at The Pas—the trading and supply center for the north—continued building the railroad northward, establishing small towns along the way. Soon trains were hauling copper and zinc ore from several mines in Flin Flon. Prospectors explored the Lynn Lake area and discovered gold, copper, and zinc. Later, nickel was found and mined in Thompson.

Workers at a Manitoba military base refuel warplanes during World War II. Many women managed farms, worked in factories, and served in the armed forces during the war.

During the 1940s, northern Manitobans mined metals for making the weapons needed by overseas troops during World War II. Some Manitobans joined the British forces fighting overseas. At home the province's farmers grew food for the troops, and Manitoba's military bases trained pilots.

After the war, more and more factories were built in Manitoba. Better paying jobs in manufacturing lured people from farms to cities. At the same time, farmers who stayed on the land now had faster new machinery, so they could run bigger farms with fewer workers.

Since the 1960s, Métis and First Nations in Manitoba have been seeking more rights. The Métis united with French-speaking peoples across Canada to make the use of the French language more widespread. Nowadays, all Canadian laws must be translated into French, and Manitobans can choose French-language classes from kindergarten all the way through college.

Manitoba's First Nations gained a strong voice in 1981. That year Chief Elijah Harper, an Ojibway-Cree from the Red Sucker Reserve, won a seat in the Manitoba Parliament. He was later elected to the Canadian House of Commons. And in 1993 Yvon Dumont became the first recent Métis to be appointed lieutenant governor of Manitoba.

Elijah Harper

With the help of leaders like Elijah Harper and Yvon Dumont, Manitobans began to realize that they had never thanked Louis Riel for his part in making Manitoba a province long ago. In 1993 Riel was formally declared one of Manitoba's founding fathers, showing the nation that Riel played a key role in uniting this province of diverse peoples.

Yvon Dumont

Canada's Crossroads

Manitoba, because of its location at the heart of the nation, is Canada's economic crossroads. Products headed for Manitoba and provinces farther west are distributed from Winnipeg. Here and at the Hudson Bay port of Churchill, goods from Manitoba and from neighboring provinces are shipped to destinations around the world. Agricultural products—especially wheat—are the most important of these **exports.**

Besides wheat, Manitoba's chief crops are barley and canola. Flax, mustard, and sunflowers are grown for their seeds, which are pressed into cooking oil. In south central Manitoba, some farmers raise garden vegetables. Beef cattle and hogs—the province's most important livestock—are raised in western Manitoba. Nine percent of the province's workers have jobs on farms.

To help preserve their fields, Manitoba's farmers use several methods to stop erosion, so that wind and water won't carry away the rich topsoil. For example, some farmers leave plant stubs

Stacks of lumber line the docks at the port in Churchill on Hudson Bay. Besides lumber, wheat and other grains are shipped from Churchill to faraway markets.

on their fields after the fall harvest to hold soil in place. Others plant grass on bare fields and invite neighboring farmers to graze livestock on these pastures. Planting shelterbelts of trees is another way that growers prevent erosion.

MIXED FARMING IN MANITOBA

In southern Manitoba, Shawne Hagan operates a mixed farm. It produces a variety of goods, including wheat, livestock feed, and cattle. As on all farms, "Work changes with the seasons," Shawne explains. "It's a year-round job, but we're busiest in the winter."

Shawne also raises horses. One of his products is horse urine, which he sells to a drug company for making medicine. Manitoba is one of the largest producers of horse urine in Canada.

In warm weather, Shawne's horses run and graze freely in the pasture. He has one stud (male) for each twenty mares (females). During the summer, the mares get pregnant. When it gets colder, they are brought into a heated barn. Pouches are attached to each mare to catch her urine, which runs into a large jug.

"Our winter chores start at 8 A.M.," says Shawne. First, the horses are fed oats and hay. Shawne and his helper then inspect the equipment and empty the urine jugs into a huge stainless steel tank. Twice a week, a truck arrives to collect the urine.

After feeding the horses, the men clean out the stalls with a front-end loader and a tractor. They stack the manure in a huge pile. (When spring arrives, they will spread it on the fields to help the crops grow.) The horses are fed again at 1 P.M. and at 5 P.M. Before dusk, they are checked again and the barn is swept. Finally, Shawne turns out the lights.

All winter long, Shawne keeps the mares and studs separate. In March he lets the mares into a large sheltered corral. Around the first of May, they start birthing their foals. By the end of June, the mares are put into the pasture again.

Like other mixed farms, Shawne's operation makes good use of farm waste. Besides using manure and selling horse urine, Shawne buys wheat stubble from other farmers. He binds the stubble into bales for the horses to eat.

Shawne has always wanted to raise horses. The animals are not only part of a valuable farm operation. They also are riding horses, and they all have names.

In addition to rich soil, Manitoba has a valuable supply of other natural resources. Minerals are an important source of wealth in the province. More than one-third of the nation's nickel (Canada's leading mineral) is mined in Manitoba. Some of the nickel is used to produce Canadian coins at the Royal Canadian Mint in Winnipeg.

Gold, copper, zinc, and silver also are found in Manitoba. While metals are unearthed up north, minerals used in construction—including limestone, gravel, sand, and gypsum—are mined in the south. Workers in the southwest drill for oil. After they have finished using a mine, companies are required to clean up the site to avoid contaminating nearby land and water supplies. Only 1 percent of the workforce is employed in mining.

Mining trucks near Thompson line up after a long day of work. Thompson is Manitoba's leading producer of nickel.

Water is one of Manitoba's most important natural resources. Covering one-sixth of the province's surface area, Manitoba's waters are used to generate 99 percent of the province's electricity. In addition, Manitoba sells some hydroelectric power to neighboring provinces and states. Rivers and lakes in Manitoba also support a vast fishery.

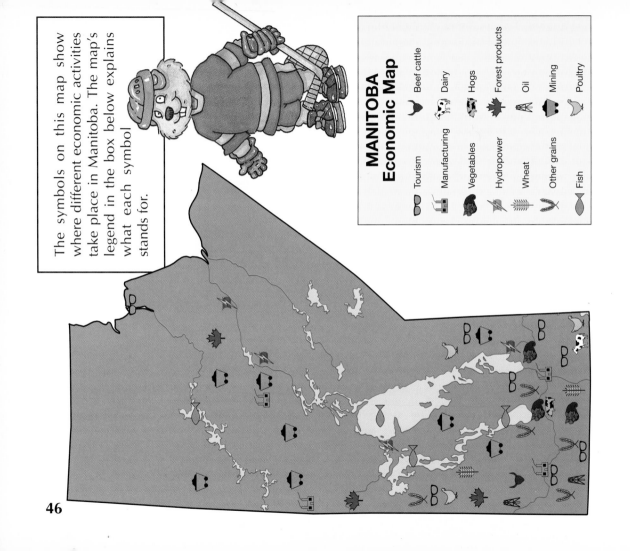

The symbols on this map show where different economic activities take place in Manitoba. The map's legend in the box below explains what each symbol stands for.

MANITOBA Economic Map

Beef cattle
Dairy
Hogs
Forest products
Oil
Mining
Poultry

Tourism
Manufacturing
Vegetables
Hydropower
Wheat
Other grains
Fish

Lakes in northern Manitoba plus Lakes Winnipeg, Manitoba, and Winnipegosis are major sources of pickerel, sauger, whitefish, and pike. Most of the catch is quick-frozen at plants throughout the province and sent to Winnipeg. From there, 90 percent of the catch is sold to cities in the northern United States.

For many communities in northern Manitoba, fishing is a source of food as well as income and employment. More than two out of three fishing licenses in Manitoba are held by Métis and First Nations people. To allow fish to continue breeding, quotas (limits) are set on how many people can fish, on how many fish can be caught, and on the length of the fishing season. Although fishers are a very small part of the province's workforce, they catch 25 percent of Canada's freshwater fish.

Some of Manitoba's natural resources are made into finished products at the province's factories. Many laborers prepare packaged meat, potato chips, frozen vegetables, soft drinks, vegetable oil, and dairy products. Others process nickel and copper. Some of the metals are shaped into finished products at factories called metalworks.

Fishing boats anchor at Gimli on the southern shore of Lake Winnipeg. Two-thirds of Manitoba's total catch of fish comes from its three largest lakes—Lakes Winnipeg, Manitoba, and Winnipegosis.

Bush pilots fly tourists and goods to northern Manitoba and carry northerners needing medical attention to hospitals in the south.

Other manufactured goods from Manitoba include buses, airplane parts, farm equipment, paper, clothing, computers, and optical fibers. Half of all the products made in Manitoba are sold outside the province—many of them to other countries. Manufacturing provides jobs for 11 percent of Manitoba's workforce.

Nowadays, most jobholders in Manitoba are part of the service industry. In fact, about three out of four workers in Manitoba hold jobs in services. This industry includes teachers, doctors, bus drivers, pilots, police officers, firefighters, and others who help people. Service workers also include store clerks and government officials.

Tourism is an important part of the service industry, too, employing about one in ten Manitobans. The more than 2 million visitors to Manitoba each year depend on people who work in hotels, campgrounds, restaurants, museums, and parks. Tourists also rely on bus drivers, train engineers, wilderness guides, and bush pilots, who fly planes to remote areas of the province.

Because of its location, Manitoba is a center for both transportation and another important service industry—trade. A network of roads and railways meets in Winnipeg, providing routes for the cattle, groceries, and wheat traded in and shipped from the province. Thousands of tons of wheat are sent by rail to Churchill, where the grain is poured onto ships headed for Europe. The airport in Winnipeg not only serves tourists but also is a cargo hub for European, Asian, and North American goods. This bustle of activity helps Manitoba live up to its nickname—the Keystone Province.

Children at the Manitoba Museum of Man and Nature in Winnipeg experiment with different types of drums. Workers at this and other museums in Manitoba have service jobs.

Manitobans come from a wide variety of ethnic backgrounds. More than 90 different ethnic groups are represented in Manitoba's population—more than in any other Canadian province.

50

The Many Faces of Manitoba

Oxcarts and steamboats once carried people to Manitoba. Nowadays, modern transportation brings people from all over the world who are drawn by Manitoba's cultural life and high-tech industries. Residents of many different backgrounds form a population that tops one million. Although the various cultures have blended over time, each group has kept its unique traditions alive.

A Manitoban competes in a dogsled race. In early times, sled dogs were used to transport mail to the north and to patrol the frontier.

Many Manitobans share a British heritage, claiming at least some English or Scottish roots. Other European backgrounds—especially Irish, German, Ukrainian, and French—are common, too. Aboriginals and Métis together make up about 7 percent of the population. Major Asian ethnic groups in Manitoba include Filippinos and Chinese. Some Manitobans trace their roots to the Caribbean, to Central and South America, or to Africa.

Only 1 out of 12 Manitobans lives in the northern four-fifths of the

A young Cree boy sits on his father's lap to listen to a traditional song.

province. With so few people, northern Manitoba has vast areas of unspoiled wilderness.

Most northern Manitobans live in mining towns, in fishing settlements, or on reserves. Large towns include The Pas, Thompson, Flin Flon, Lynn Lake, Leaf Rapids, and Gillam. Few roads are paved, and transportation between communities can be difficult. People traveling to Churchill, for example, must take the train or fly. In winter people use frozen lakes as roads and travel by snowmobile.

The rest of the population lives in southern Manitoba. The south is home to the province's two largest cities—Winnipeg and Brandon. Other large towns in the south include Portage la Prairie, Steinbach, Winkler, Selkirk, and Dauphin.

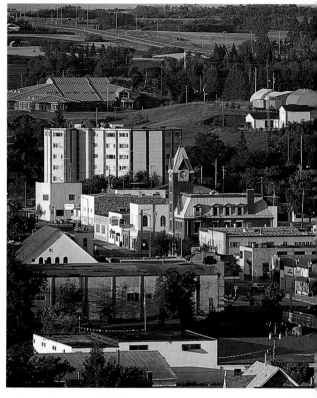

Minnedosa, a small town just north of Brandon, serves the region's grain and livestock farmers.

More than one-third of Manitoba's First Nations people live in Winnipeg. The Chipewyan, Saulteaux, and Cree also are spread throughout the province on 61 reserves. Major reserves include Opaskwayak (The Pas), Mathias Colomb (Pukatawagan), Norway House, and Peguis.

Aboriginal beadwork—colorful patterns sewn on moccasins and clothing—is popular throughout Manitoba. Paintings and prints by Native artists in the province portray Aboriginal spirits and symbols. Non-Aboriginals can visit sweat lodges—traditional steam baths used for healing and other ceremonies. Powwows, or ceremonial gatherings, welcome visitors to help celebrate Plains Indian life.

Métis fiddling and step dancing (jigging), beaded costumes, and unique food are highlights at the Festival du Voyageur. Held in Saint Boniface, Winnipeg's French-speaking district, this

Youngsters look on as hot maple syrup is poured onto snow to make maple candy during the Festival du Voyageur.

A Mennonite woman and her daughters enjoy a carnival ride in southern Manitoba.

winter event also features ice sculpting and dogsled racing. Besides those in Winnipeg, Métis live in many of Manitoba's northern communities.

Mennonites live in southern farming communities such as Steinbach, Winkler, and Altona. Known for their choirs and singing as well as for their hard work and successful farming, Mennonites celebrate their heritage at the Steinbach Pioneer Days. At this festival, and at the Mennonite Heritage Village in Steinbach, visitors can see what life was like for early settlers from Russia.

Filippinos, Vietnamese, and Cambodians are newcomers to Manitoba's Asian community. The Chinese were actually the first Asians to come to Manitoba. They built a large neighborhood in Winnipeg called Chinatown, where they bought and sold Chinese goods.

Nowadays, Winnipeg's Chinese Community and Cultural Centre helps Chinese immigrants adapt to Manitoba's cold climate, learn English, and adjust to a very different culture. Classes in Mandarin language, dance, watercolor painting, and calligraphy are also taught here.

Many Ukrainians have settled in Winnipeg and between Lakes Winnipeg and Manitoba. The onion-shaped domes of Ukrainian churches dot the Winnipeg skyline. In the city, the Ukrainian Cultural and Educational Centre and the Russalka Dancers help keep Ukrainian traditions alive. The

Chinese women in traditional dress perform during Folklorama, a multicultural festival held in Winnipeg.

Ethnic Ukrainians dance at Canada's National Ukrainian Festival in Dauphin. More than 1 in 10 Manitobans has Ukrainian ancestors.

town of Dauphin holds Canada's National Ukrainian Festival each August. At this event, Manitobans from all backgrounds enjoy music, special foods, and fancy Ukrainian Easter eggs.

Many people from Manitoba's Icelandic community have settled in Winnipeg. In nearby Gimli, Icelanders celebrate a festival called Islendingadagurinn with a parade, music, and food. On Hecla Island in Lake Winnipeg, visitors can tour a replica of an early Icelandic fishing village.

Manitobans who came from England, Scotland, and Ireland have also left their mark on Manitoba's culture. They helped create the world-famous Royal Winnipeg Ballet, the Winnipeg Symphony, and the Manitoba Opera Association.

The Forks, a shopping and gathering place in Winnipeg, features a public market, concerts, festivals, and natural areas for hiking, ice skating, and cross-country skiing.

Winnipeg is well known as a shopping district and a cultural center for ballet, opera, symphony, and theater. Each August the capital hosts a two-week multicultural festival called Folklorama. In pavilions around the city, people sample food, music, dance, and handicrafts from 40 different countries.

A variety of activities draws many people beyond Winnipeg. Festivals such as the Winnipeg Folk Festival in nearby Birds Hill, the Thresherman's Reunion and Stampede in Austin, the Firefighter's Rodeo in Virden, and the Northern Manitoba Trappers' Festival in The Pas are popular. Many people also take advantage of Manitoba's great outdoors. For example, Lake Winnipeg's Grand Beach is considered one of the top 10 beaches in North America because of its soft powdery sand.

A kayaker paddles down the Nelson River in northern Manitoba. Manitoba's vast wilderness offers outdoor adventurers plenty of fun activities.

Some Manitobans enjoy observing wildlife—polar bears and whales in Churchill, elks and wolves in Riding Mountain National Park, great gray owls and other birds throughout the province. Adventurers climb Baldy Mountain in Duck Mountain Provincial Park. Hikers, canoeists, and fishers retreat to several provincial parks, including Whiteshell and Atikaki in the Canadian Shield region.

Manitobans are also big sports fans. They follow the Winnipeg Blue Bombers in football and the Winnipeg Jets in hockey. The province's long winters have helped make Manitobans hockey and curling champions. Every town has a rink reserved for hockey, curling, and skating. The tough climate has made Manitobans strong and independent—they have to be to survive and prosper in their great northern paradise!

Famous Manitobans

■ **Jackson Beardy** (1944–1984), from Island Lake, Manitoba, painted many images from Native Cree legends. His artwork is displayed in several countries and has been sold worldwide.

2 **Gordon Bell** (1863–1923) was Manitoba's first bacteriologist, a scientist who identifies and studies bacteria, or germs. To help stop the spread of disease-causing bacteria, Bell set up standards for milk and for cleaning up Winnipeg's housing and sewage systems.

3 **Sylvia Burka** (born 1954), from Winnipeg, overcame the loss of an eye in a childhood accident to compete internationally in two sports—skating and bicycling. The fastest female speed skater in the world through most of the 1980s, Burka won five national titles and was named Canadian Skater of the Year six times.

4 **Len Cariou** (born 1939), from Saint Boniface, Manitoba, is a famous actor, singer, and director who started his career on Winnipeg's Rainbow Stage and at the Manitoba Theatre Centre. He is often seen on television in *Murder She Wrote*.

■ **Bruce Chown** (1893–1986), a doctor from Winnipeg, is known around the world as a lifesaver of newborn babies. Through his research, Chown discovered the clue that helped prevent brain damage and death from Rh disease, a blood condition that destroys red blood cells.

6 **Bobby Clarke** (born 1949) grew up playing hockey in his hometown of Flin Flon, Manitoba. While he was captain of the Philadelphia Flyers during the 1970s, they won two Stanley Cups. Since his retirement in 1984, Clarke has managed the Flyers and other U.S. hockey teams. In 1987 he was elected to the U.S. Hockey Hall of Fame.

7 **Crash Test Dummies,** a rock band from Manitoba, has sold more than 4 million records worldwide. The group includes four members from Winnipeg—**Brad Roberts** (born 1964), **Dan Roberts** (born 1967), **Ben Darvell** (born 1967), and **Mitch Dordge** (born 1960)—along with **Ellen Reid** (born 1966) from Selkirk, Manitoba.

8 **Tracy Dahl** (born 1961) wanted to be an actress before she began singing with the Manitoba Opera in 1982. Since then, the Winnipeg native has been a guest artist in operas and musicals around the world.

9 **Evelyn Hart** (born 1956) has been the star dancer of the Royal Winnipeg Ballet since 1979. In 1980 she became the first Canadian to win a gold medal at the International Ballet Competition in Bulgaria. Born in Ontario, Hart received the Order of Canada in 1983 and was named Manitoba's Woman of the Year in 1987.

■ **Tomson Highway** (born 1951), from Brochet, Manitoba, writes plays about life on reserves. *The Rez Sisters* and *Dry Lips Oughta Move to Kapuskasing* have won awards and have been staged all across Canada.

11 **E. Cora Hind** (1861–1942) moved in 1881 from Ontario to Winnipeg, where she wrote reports on agriculture for the *Manitoba Free Press*. The first female journalist in western Canada, Hind gained quick fame for her accurate forecasts of wheat crop yields, a skill that affected the prices traders paid and farmers earned for the grain.

12 **John Hirsch** (1930–1990), originally from Hungary, moved to Winnipeg in 1947. There he founded the Muddiwater Puppets and the Manitoba Theatre Centre, the first permanent professional theater in western Canada. Hirsch won many awards for his artistic work.

61

■ **Tom Jackson** (born 1949), a singer and actor based in Winnipeg, regularly appears on the PBS children's show *Shining Time Station*. He's also played major roles in the CBC television series *North of 60* and in the CBC movies *The Diviners* and *Medicine River*. From his acting career Jackson raises money to help the poor. Of English-Cree descent, Jackson has also produced a musical about First Nations life called *Dreamcatcher*.

■ **Tom Lamb** (1898–1969) learned wilderness survival skills as a youth in northern Manitoba. Born in Grand Rapids, Manitoba, Lamb started the airline Lambair in 1935. A trapper, logger, and businessman, he flew geologists to remote areas of the province to explore for minerals.

15 **Margaret Laurence** (1926–1987), from Neepawa, Manitoba, was Canada's first internationally known author. Her books—including *A Jest of God* and *The Stone Angel*—told the stories of Hagar Shipley and other Manitoba prairie women.

16 **Gweneth Lloyd** (1901–1993) moved from England to Winnipeg in 1938 to found the ballet company that grew into the Royal Winnipeg Ballet. A dancer, choreographer (creator of dance moves), and teacher, Lloyd made the company world famous.

17 **Carol Matas** (born 1949), a Winnipeg author of young-adult titles, has won awards for her books, including *Lisa, Adventure in Legoland, Sworn Enemies,* and *The Burning Time*.

18 **Fred Penner** (born 1947), a children's entertainer from Winnipeg, is famous for "The Cat Came Back" and other popular songs. He has sold more than 1 million records and stars in his own television show—*Fred Penner's Place*. Books based on his songs are *The Bump, Ebeneezer Sneezer,* and *Roller Skating*. In 1992 he received the Order of Canada.

19 James A. Richardson (1885–1939) became president of his family's company, James Richardson and Sons, Ltd., in 1919. He guided the Winnipeg company to become one of Canada's largest grain and investment firms. Richardson also served as president of the Winnipeg Grain Exchange and started Western Canadian Airways and Canadian Airways, gaining the nickname the Father of Commercial Aviation in Canada.

20 Gabrielle Roy (1909–1983), born in Saint Boniface, Manitoba, wrote books about growing up on the prairie as a poor girl of French heritage. One of Canada's most important writers, Roy won several literary prizes. Many of her books, including *The Tin Flute,* have been translated from French into English and other languages.

■ **David Schellenberg** (1832–1911) came to Manitoba with a group of Mennonites from Russia in 1878. Sometimes called the Father of Rural Tree Planting, Schellenberg began the practice of planting shelterbelts on the treeless prairies of southern Manitoba.

22 Edward Richard Schreyer (born 1935), from Beauséjour, Manitoba, became the youngest member of the province's legislature at the age of 22. By age 33, he had become Manitoba's premier. He went on to serve as governor general of Canada and as Canadian high commissioner to Australia.

23 Baldur Stefansson (born 1917), from Vestfold, Manitoba, is known as the Father of Canola. A plant scientist, he developed rapeseed into a less-acidic, edible crop called canola—now one of Canada's leading crops—grown for its oil. In 1985 Stefansson received the Order of Canada.

Fast Facts

Provincial Symbols

Nickname: Keystone Province
Flower: prairie crocus
Bird: great gray owl
Tartan: red for the Red River Settlement, green for natural resources, blue for Lord Selkirk (founder of the Red River Colony), dark green for the men and women of many races who have enriched Manitoba, and gold for grain and other agricultural products

Provincial Highlights

Landmarks: Atikaki Provincial Wilderness Park, Duck Mountain Provincial Park, Spruce Woods Provincial Park, Grand Beach, Boychuk Ukrainian Museum in Rossburn, Hecla Village, Grant's Old Mill and the Royal Canadian Mint in Winnipeg, Mennonite Heritage Village in Steinbach, York Factory National Historic Site

Annual events: Northern Manitoba Trappers' Festival in The Pas (Feb.), Winnipeg International Children's Festival (June), Winnipeg Folk Festival (July), Canadian Turtle Derby in Boissevain (July), Nickel Days in Thompson (July), Frog Jumping Championships in Saint Pierre-Jolys (Aug.), Opaskwayak Indian Days in The Pas (Aug.), Ag-Ex Manitoba in Brandon (Oct.)

Professional sports teams: Winnipeg Jets (hockey), Winnipeg Blue Bombers (football), Winnipeg Fury (soccer), Winnipeg Gold Eyes (baseball)

Population

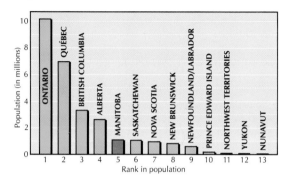

Population*: 1,092,000
Rank in population, nationwide: 5th
Population distribution: 72 percent urban; 28 percent rural
Population density: 5.2 people per sq mi (2 per sq km)
Capital: Winnipeg (616,790)
Major cities and towns (and populations*): Brandon (38,573), Thompson (14,977), Portage la Prairie (13,186), Selkirk (9,815), Dauphin (8,453), Steinbach (8,213), Flin Flon (7,119)
Major ethnic groups*: multiple backgrounds, 38 percent; British, 17 percent; German, 9 percent; Ukrainian, 7 percent; Aboriginal and French, 5 percent each; Métis, Dutch, and Polish, 2 percent each; Italian and Scandinavian, 1 percent each; other single origins, 11 percent
*1991 census

Endangered Species
Birds: anatum peregrine falcon, piping plover, loggerhead shrike
Plants: small white lady's slipper, western fringed prairie orchid

Geographic Highlights
Area (land/water): 250,946 sq mi (649,950 sq km)
Rank in area, nationwide: 8th
Highest point: Baldy Mountain (2,730 ft/832 m)
Major lakes: Winnipeg, Winnipegosis, Manitoba, Southern Indian, Cedar, Island, Gods
Major rivers: Assiniboine, Red, Nelson

Economy
Percentage of Workers Per Job Sector

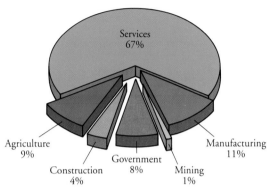

Services 67%
Agriculture 9%
Construction 4%
Government 8%
Mining 1%
Manufacturing 11%

Natural resources: fresh water, forests, wildlife, fertile soils, cobalt, copper, gold, nickel, zinc, gypsum, limestone, petroleum, potash

Agricultural products: wheat, barley, canola, flaxseed, mustard seed, sunflowers, oats, potatoes, rye, vegetables, beef and dairy cattle, chickens, eggs, hogs

Manufactured goods: packaged meat, canned and frozen vegetables, dairy products, livestock feed, soft drinks, vegetable oil, aerospace equipment, buses, newspapers, electrical equipment, primary metal, computer parts, telecommunications equipment, clothing, machine tools, structural metal, agricultural equipment

Energy
Electric power: hydroelectric (99 percent), fuel-burning (1 percent)

65

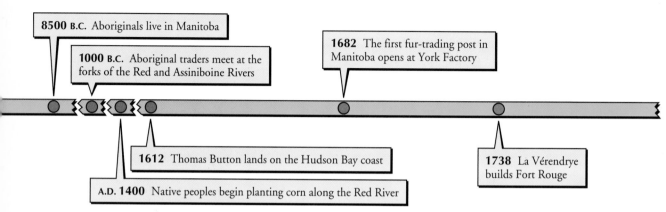

8500 B.C. Aboriginals live in Manitoba

1000 B.C. Aboriginal traders meet at the forks of the Red and Assiniboine Rivers

1682 The first fur-trading post in Manitoba opens at York Factory

1612 Thomas Button lands on the Hudson Bay coast

A.D. 1400 Native peoples begin planting corn along the Red River

1738 La Vérendrye builds Fort Rouge

Federal Government

Capital: Ottawa

Head of state: British Crown, represented by the governor general

Head of government: prime minister

Cabinet: ministers appointed by the prime minister

Parliament: Senate—104 members appointed by the governor general; House of Commons—295 members elected by the people

Manitoba representation in parliament: 6 senators; 14 house members

Voting age: 18

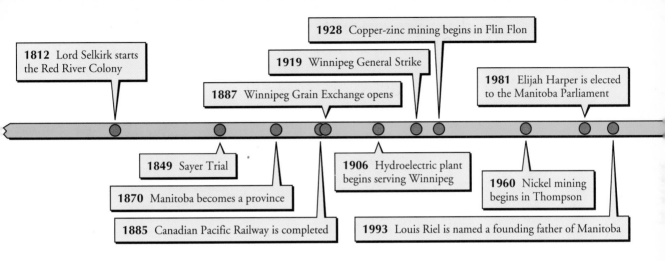

1812 Lord Selkirk starts the Red River Colony

1887 Winnipeg Grain Exchange opens

1919 Winnipeg General Strike

1928 Copper-zinc mining begins in Flin Flon

1981 Elijah Harper is elected to the Manitoba Parliament

1849 Sayer Trial

1870 Manitoba becomes a province

1885 Canadian Pacific Railway is completed

1906 Hydroelectric plant begins serving Winnipeg

1960 Nickel mining begins in Thompson

1993 Louis Riel is named a founding father of Manitoba

Provincial Government

Capital: Winnipeg
Crown representative: lieutenant governor
Head of government: premier
Cabinet: ministers appointed by the premier
Legislative Assembly: 57 members elected to terms that can last up to five years
Voting age: 18 years
Major political parties: New Democratic, Progressive Conservative, Liberal

Government Services

To help pay the people who work for Manitoba's government, Manitobans pay taxes on money they earn and on many of the items they buy. The services run by the provincial government help assure Manitobans of a high quality of life. Government funds pay for medical care, for education, for road building and repairs, and for other facilities such as libraries and parks. In addition, the government has funds to help people who are disabled, elderly, or poor.

Glossary

colony   A territory ruled by a country some distance away.

escarpment   A ridge, or belt, of hilly land.

export   In trade, a product sold from one country to another.

glacier   A large body of ice and snow that moves slowly over land.

hydroelectric power   The electricity produced by using the force of flowing water. Also called hydropower.

ice age   A period when glaciers cover large regions of the earth's surface. The term *Ice Age* usually refers to the most recent one, called the Pleistocene, which began almost 2 million years ago and ended about 10,000 years ago.

immigrant   A person who moves into a foreign country and settles there.

muskeg   A mossy bog, or wetland, that contains thick layers of decayed plant matter. Muskegs are often found in northern Canada.

northern lights   A strange and sometimes colorful light display seen in dark night skies in northern lands. Sometimes the lights form a still arc; other times they form streamers that constantly change shape. Also called aurora borealis.

permafrost   Ground that remains frozen below the surface for two or more years.

prairie A large area of level or gently rolling grassy land with few trees.

precipitation Rain, snow, and other forms of moisture that fall to earth.

reserve Public land set aside by the government to be used by Native peoples.

tundra A treeless plain found in arctic and subarctic regions. The ground is permanently frozen, except for a thin top layer that thaws in summer, allowing mosses, lichens, and short shrubs to grow.

Index

About the Author

Sarah Yates has been a professional writer for more than 20 years. Author of various children's books, including *Can't You Be Still?* and *Nobody Knows!,* Ms. Yates loves writing for children because they are such an honest and demanding audience. She also practices puppetry. Ms. Yates lives in Winnipeg with her daughter, Gemma, and her artist-husband, Ted.

Acknowledgments

Laura Westlund, pp. 1, 3, 64, 65 (right), 66–67; Mapping Specialists Ltd., pp. 12–13, 46; Brian Sytnyk/Vis-U-Tel Photography, pp. 2, 8, 9, 10, 14, 15, 17, 18 (both), 19, 21, 23, 43, 44 (background), 45, 48, 50 (all), 51, 52, 53, 54, 55, 56, 57, 58, 59, 68, 69, 71; Artwork by Terry Boles, pp. 6, 12, 46, 65; Gerry Lemmo, p. 7; Jerry Hennen, pp. 11, 47; Sandy Black, pp. 16, 20; The Forks Public Archaeology Project, p. 24; National Archives of Canada, pp. 25 (C-114467-detail), 27 (C-1917), 28 (C-6896), 32 (C-13965), 35 (C-56472), 37 (C-6605); Provincial Archives of Manitoba, pp. 29 (Hudson's Bay Company Archives), 30 (N-8755), 33 (N-12577), 36 (N-16116), 39, 40, 60 (top right: N-10084), 61 (bottom left: N-978), 61 (bottom right), 63 (center right: N-13920); Artwork by John Erste, p. 31; Saskatchewan Archives Board, p. 34 (R-A2294); Studio von deelong, p. 41 (top); Manitoba Government, p. 41 (bottom); Manitoba Museum of Man and Nature, p. 49; Canadian Amateur Speed Skating Association, p. 60 (center left); Hollywood Book and Poster, p. 60 (bottom left); © Ed Mahan Photo/Philadelphia Flyers, p. 60 (bottom right); Timothy White, p. 61 (top right); © Lisa Kohler, p. 61 (center left); Royal Winnipeg Ballet, pp. 61 (center right: photo by Paul Martens), 62 (center right); David Laurence, p. 62 (top right); Peter Tittenberger, p. 62 (center left); Albert Cheung, p. 62 (bottom right); James Richardson and Sons, Ltd., p. 63 (top left); La Société historique de Saint-Boniface, p. 63 (center left); Department of Archives and Special Collections, The University of Manitoba, p. 63 (bottom left); Gerry Kopelow/Photographics, Inc., p. 72.